"Mr. People"

all about drawing people

Written and Illustrated by

Mason Mitchell

Outskirts Press, Inc.
Denver, Colorado

"Mr. People" is an educational drawing book on how to draw people. It was written and illustrated for children seven years old and older, the non and beginning artist. (Adults will enjoy it too.) It is an easy systematic drawing technique based off of what I call the spinning top shape, which is a fun new and innovative way of drawing people. The book is divided into three main drawing sections: (1) drawing the head and face, (2) drawing the body, and (3) action drawing.

(1) Drawing the Head and Face

This introductory section is a preparatory exercise that will be applied later. Here, we start with the basic circle for the human head. Incorporate the use of the "T", horizontal lines, dots and halves for facial features. Next, we progress to a drawn circle of any type using the same technique for facial features as we did in the basic circle. This progression is done in a step-by-step process that produces an amazing variety of people.

(2) Drawing the Body

In this section, we draw Mr. People and other people's body by using a step-by-step drawing technique. As well as adding the facial lessons we learned in section (1). In this section one is able to draw front views, rear views and side views of a variety of people. One will be able to draw tall, short, big, and thin people with incredible ease.

(3) Action Drawing

Using the technique introduced in Section 1 and 2, movement is given to the figures.

(4) Drawing Exercises

CONTENTS

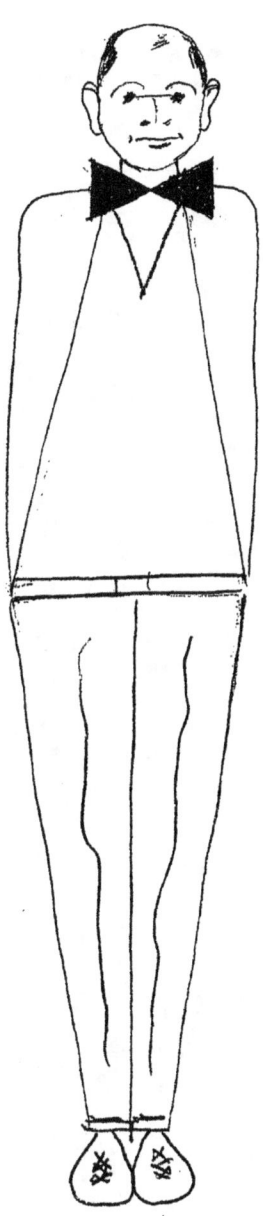

Hi,
I'm Mr. People

Welcome to a fun
New way of
Drawing People

Drawing
Head and Faces

Let's Begin

By Drawing a
Basic Face
Technique

Draw a circle
of any shape

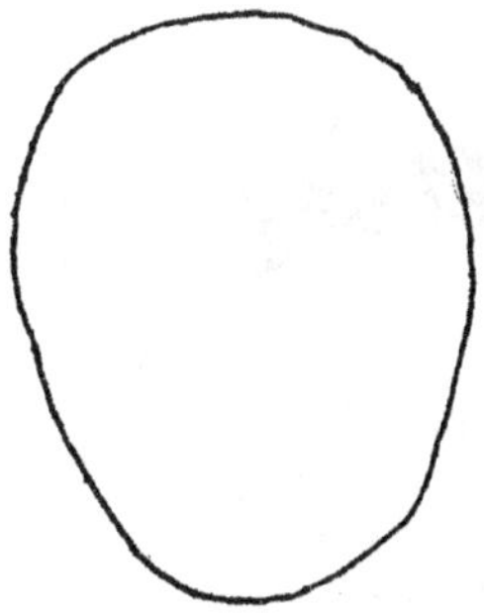

Draw a capital
"T" in the Middle
of the Face

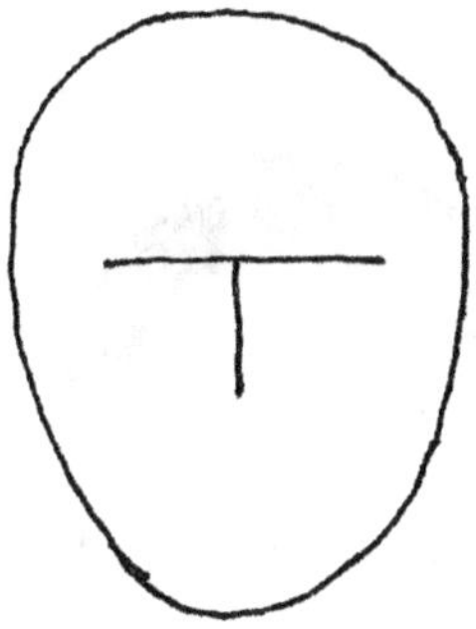

Add 1/2 a heart
for ears

Two (2) Horizontal
lines for mouth

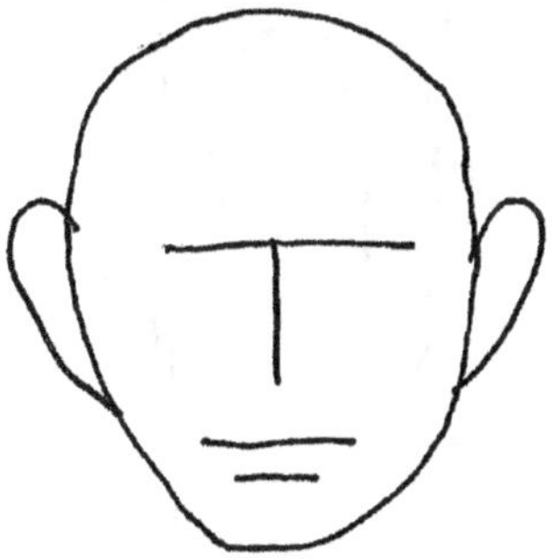

Shade in the Eyes
and Nose

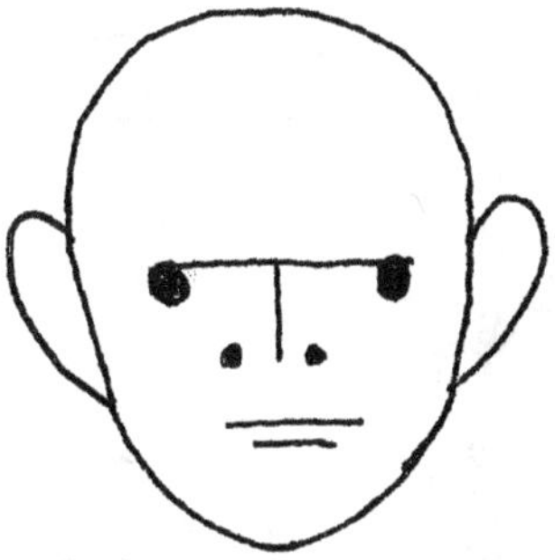

Add Eyebrows
and lines to Ears

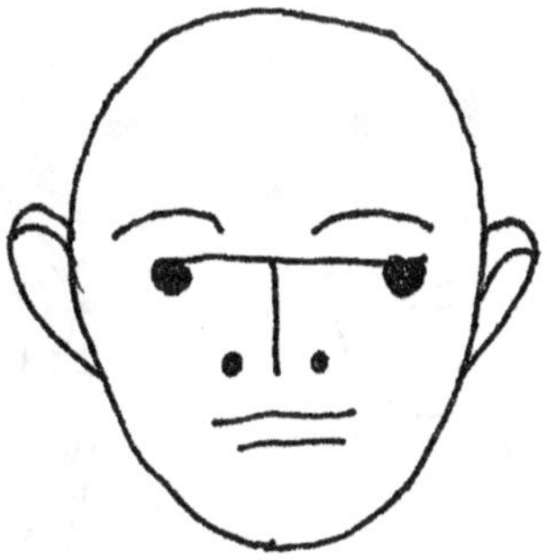

Practice Space

13

Faces come in all shapes and sizes.
Draw a circle and add your features

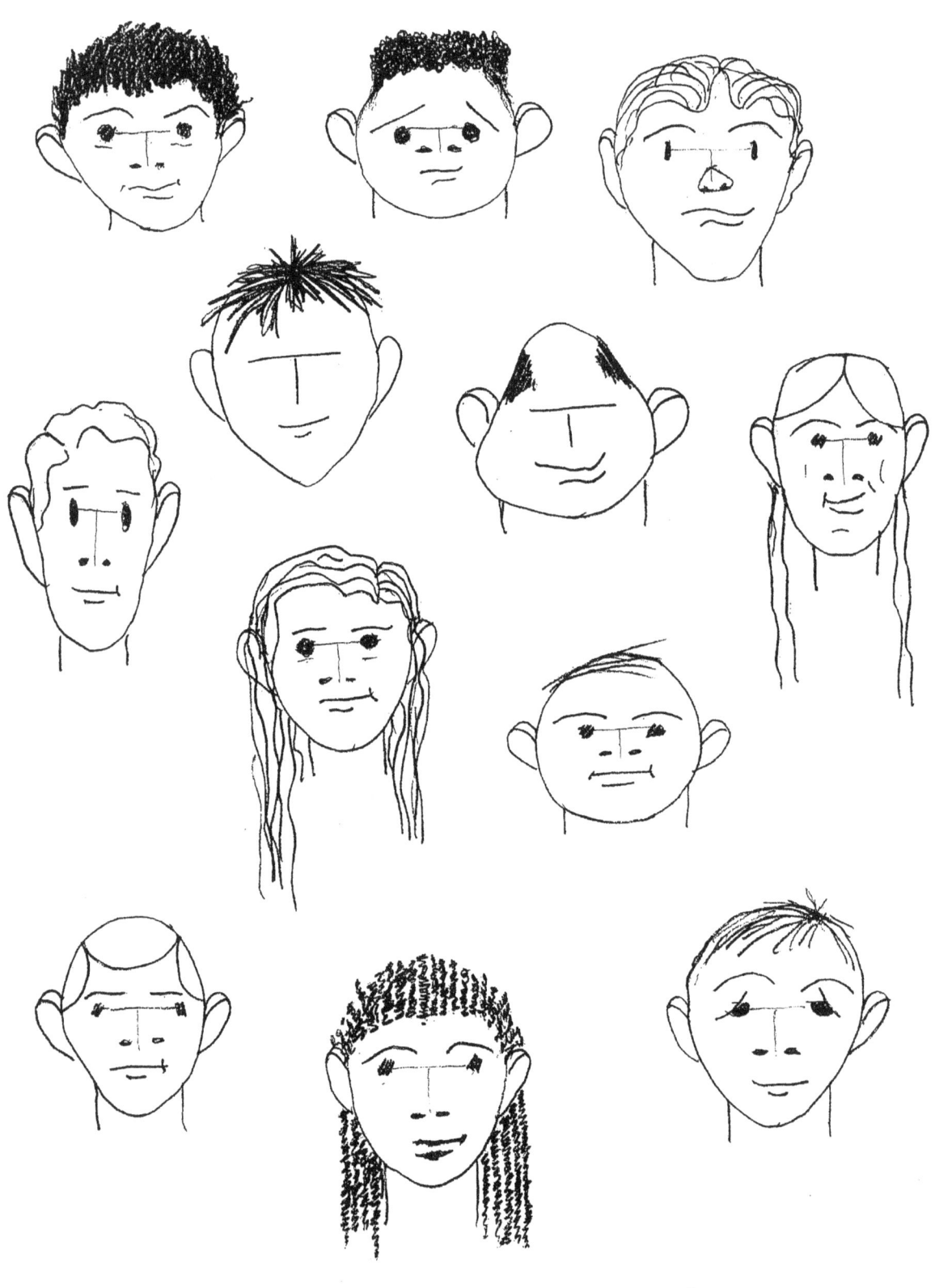

14

Practice Space

Drawing
Mr. People

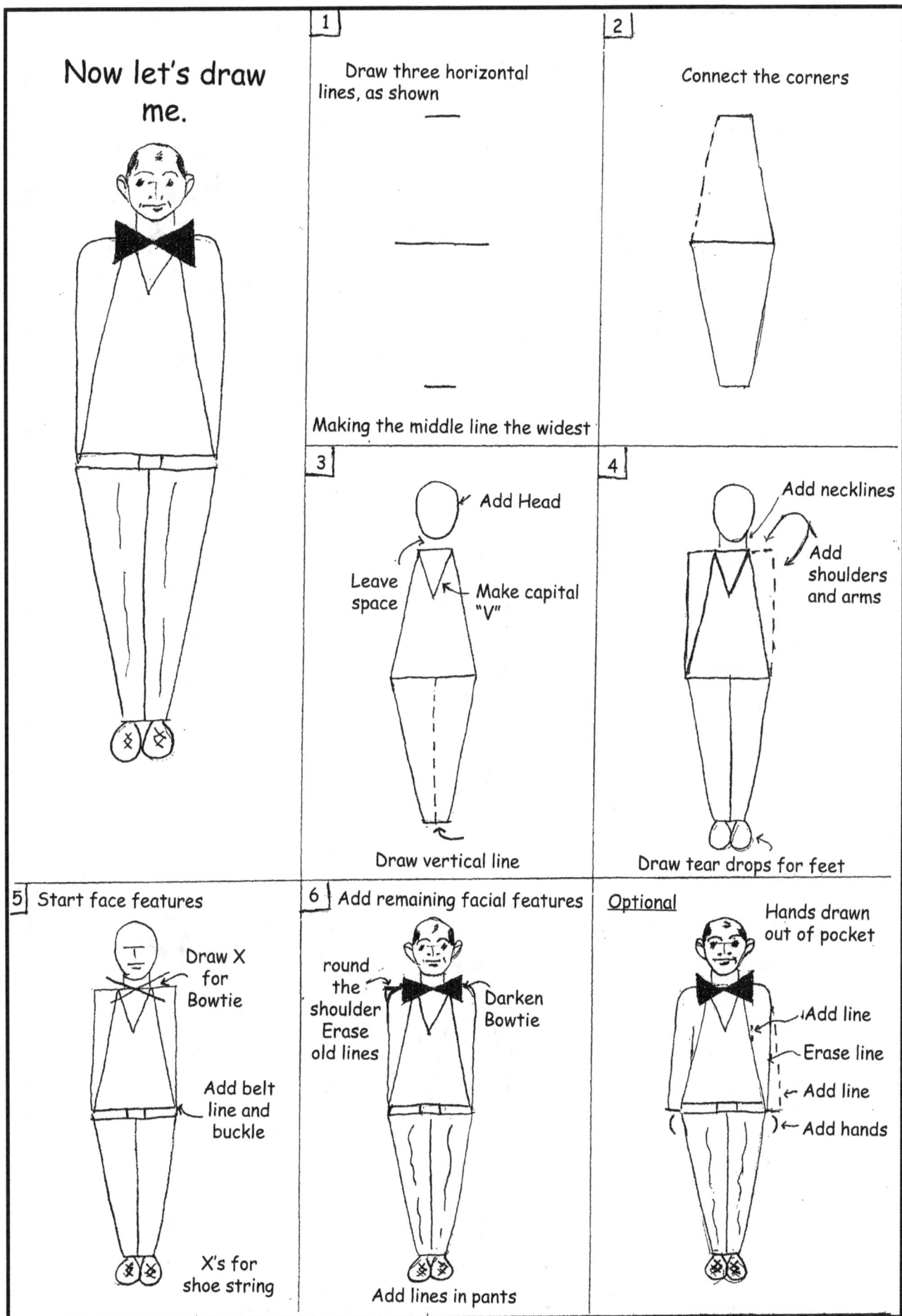

Now let's draw me.

1 Draw three horizontal lines, as shown

Making the middle line the widest

2 Connect the corners

3 Add Head

Leave space

Make capital "V"

Draw vertical line

4 Add necklines

Add shoulders and arms

Draw tear drops for feet

5 Start face features

Draw X for Bowtie

Add belt line and buckle

X's for shoe string

6 Add remaining facial features

round the shoulder Erase old lines

Darken Bowtie

Add lines in pants

Optional

Hands drawn out of pocket

Add line

Erase line

Add line

Add hands

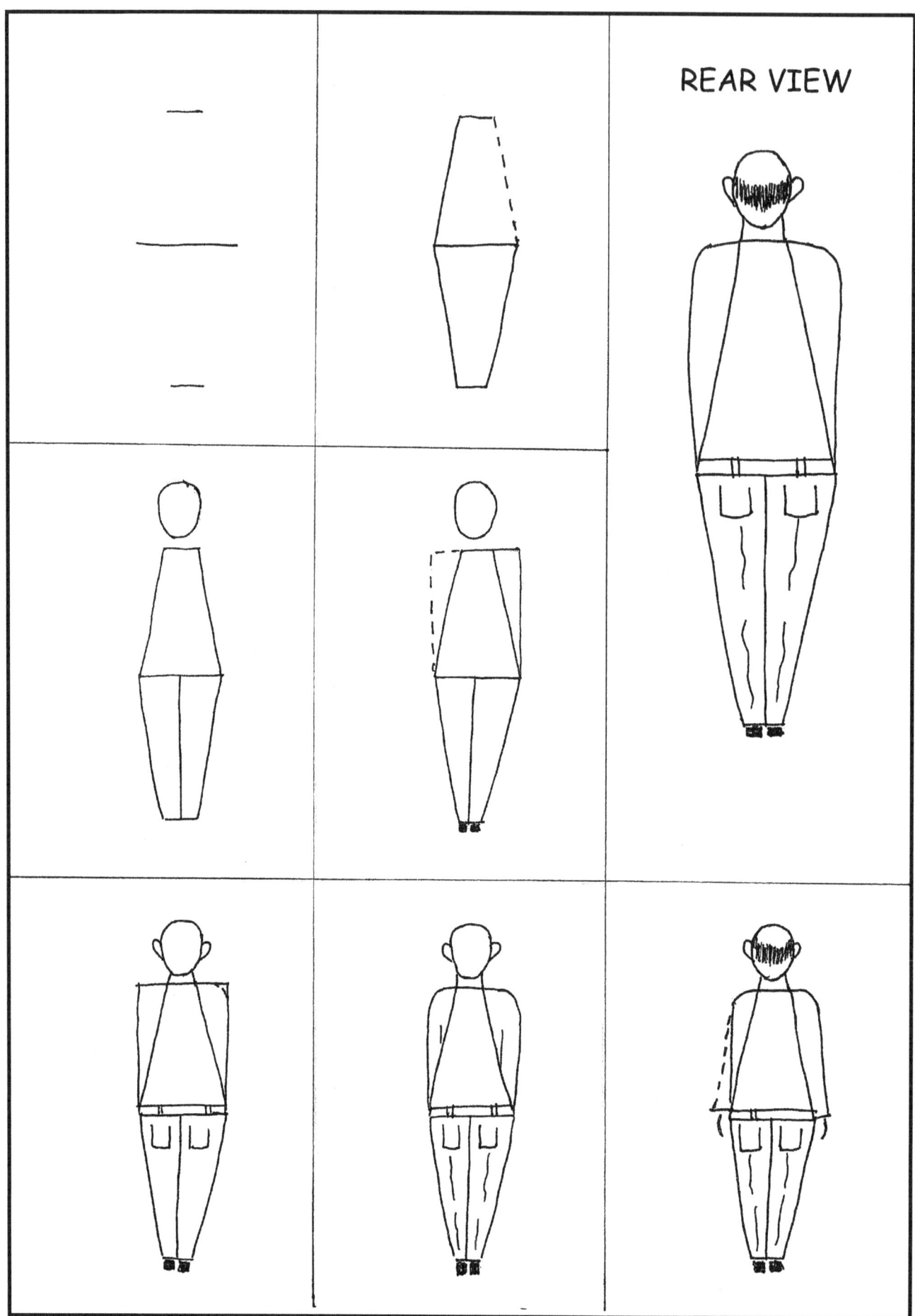

REAR VIEW

20

Drawing
The Body

In the World

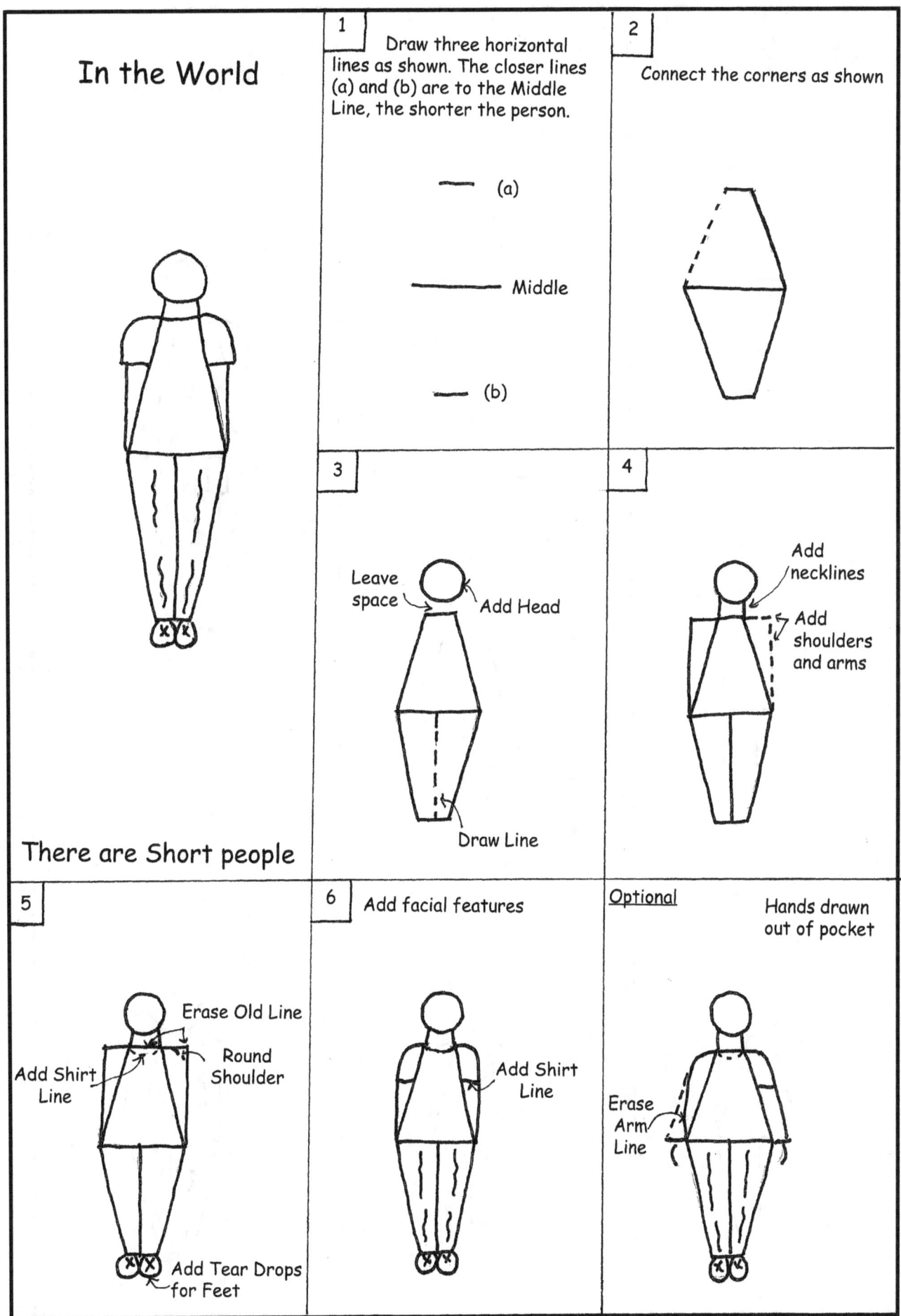

There are Short people

1 Draw three horizontal lines as shown. The closer lines (a) and (b) are to the Middle Line, the shorter the person.

— (a)

——— Middle

— (b)

2 Connect the corners as shown

3 Leave space ⌒ Add Head

Draw Line

4 Add necklines

Add shoulders and arms

5 Erase Old Line

Round Shoulder

Add Shirt Line

Add Tear Drops for Feet

6 Add facial features

Add Shirt Line

Optional Hands drawn out of pocket

Erase Arm Line

23

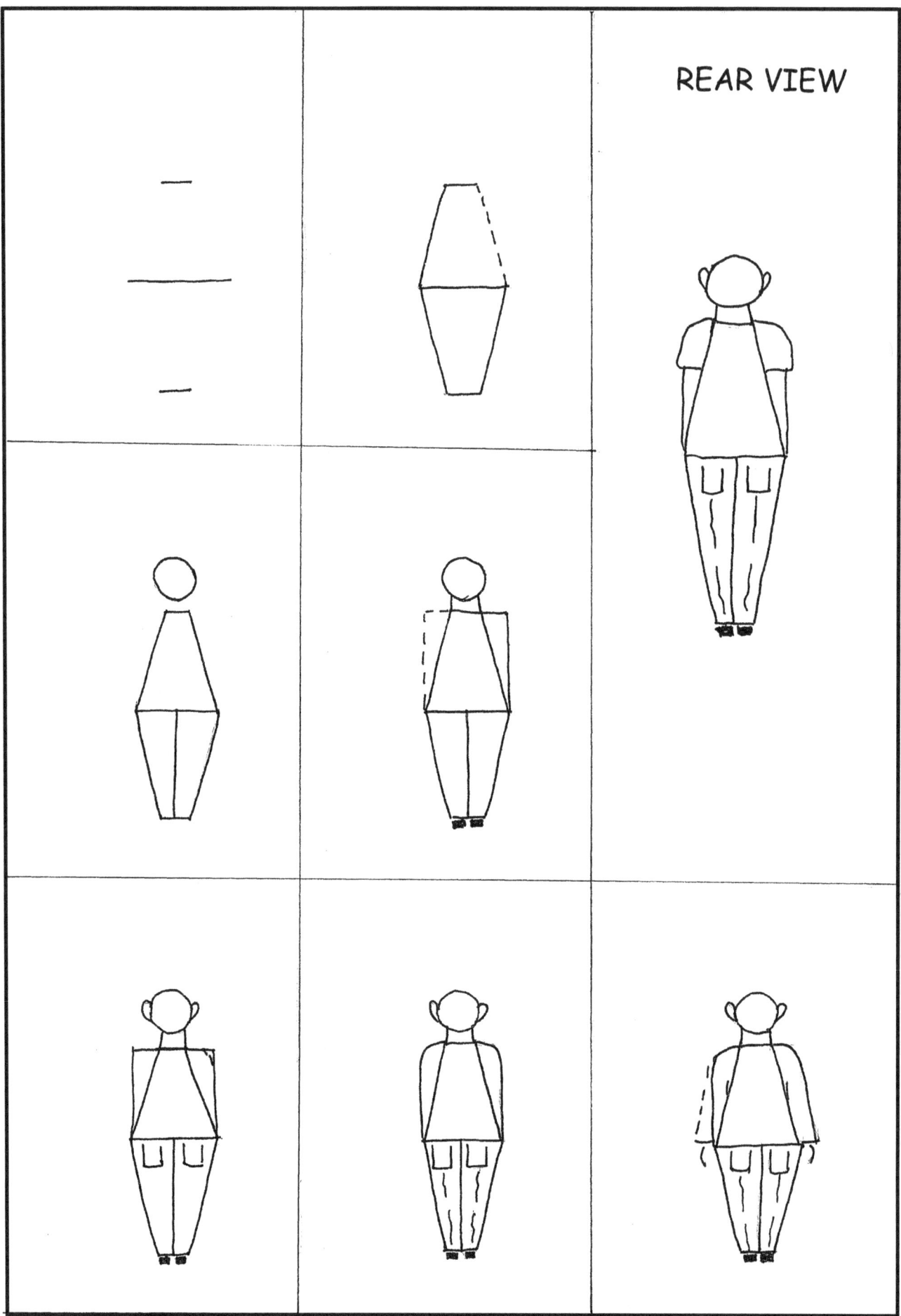

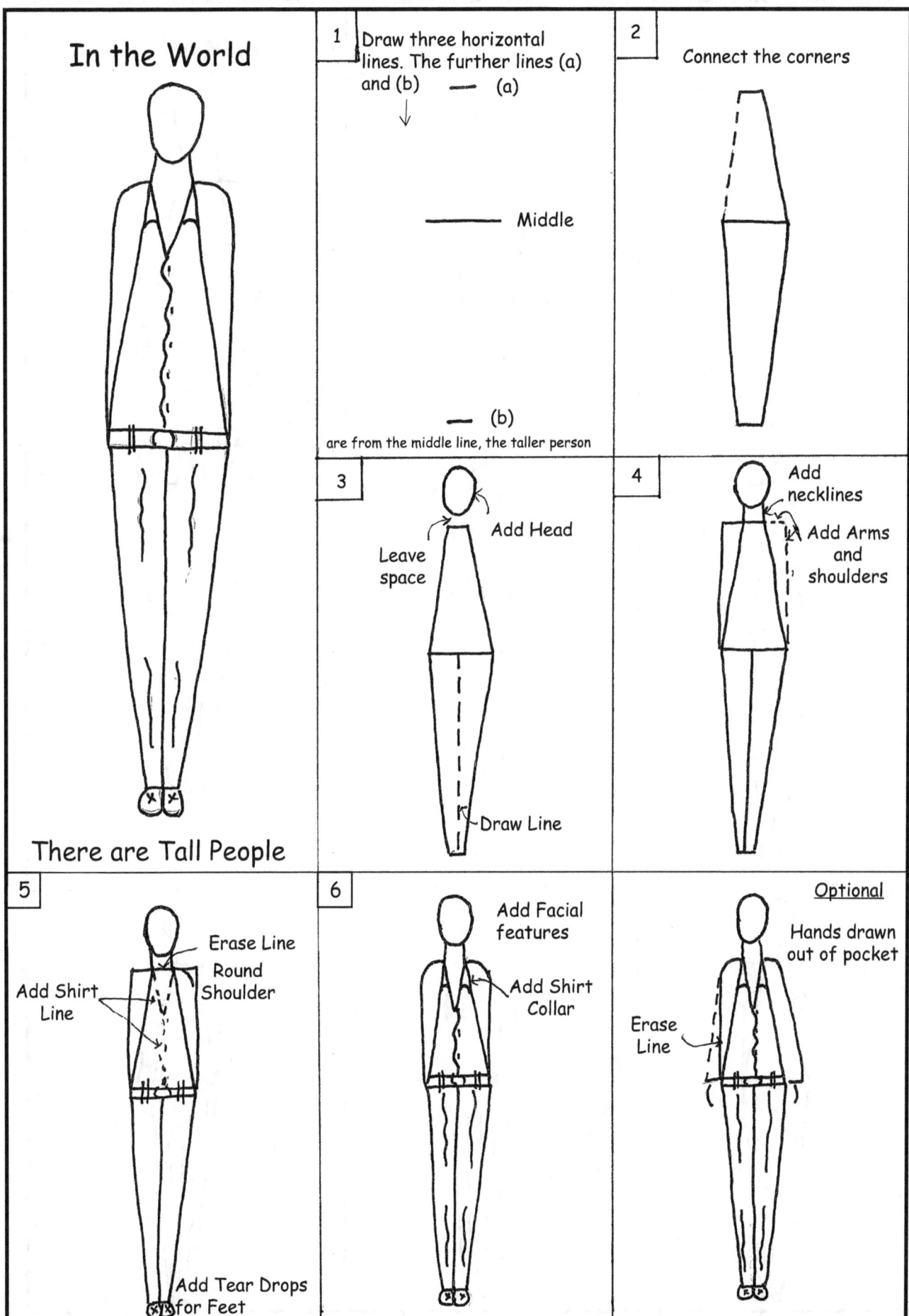

In the World

There are Tall People

1 Draw three horizontal lines. The further lines (a) and (b) ——— (a)
↓

——— Middle

——— (b)

are from the middle line, the taller person

2 Connect the corners

3 Add Head

Leave space

Draw Line

4 Add necklines

Add Arms and shoulders

5 Erase Line Round Shoulder

Add Shirt Line

Add Tear Drops for Feet

6 Add Facial features

Add Shirt Collar

Optional

Hands drawn out of pocket

Erase Line

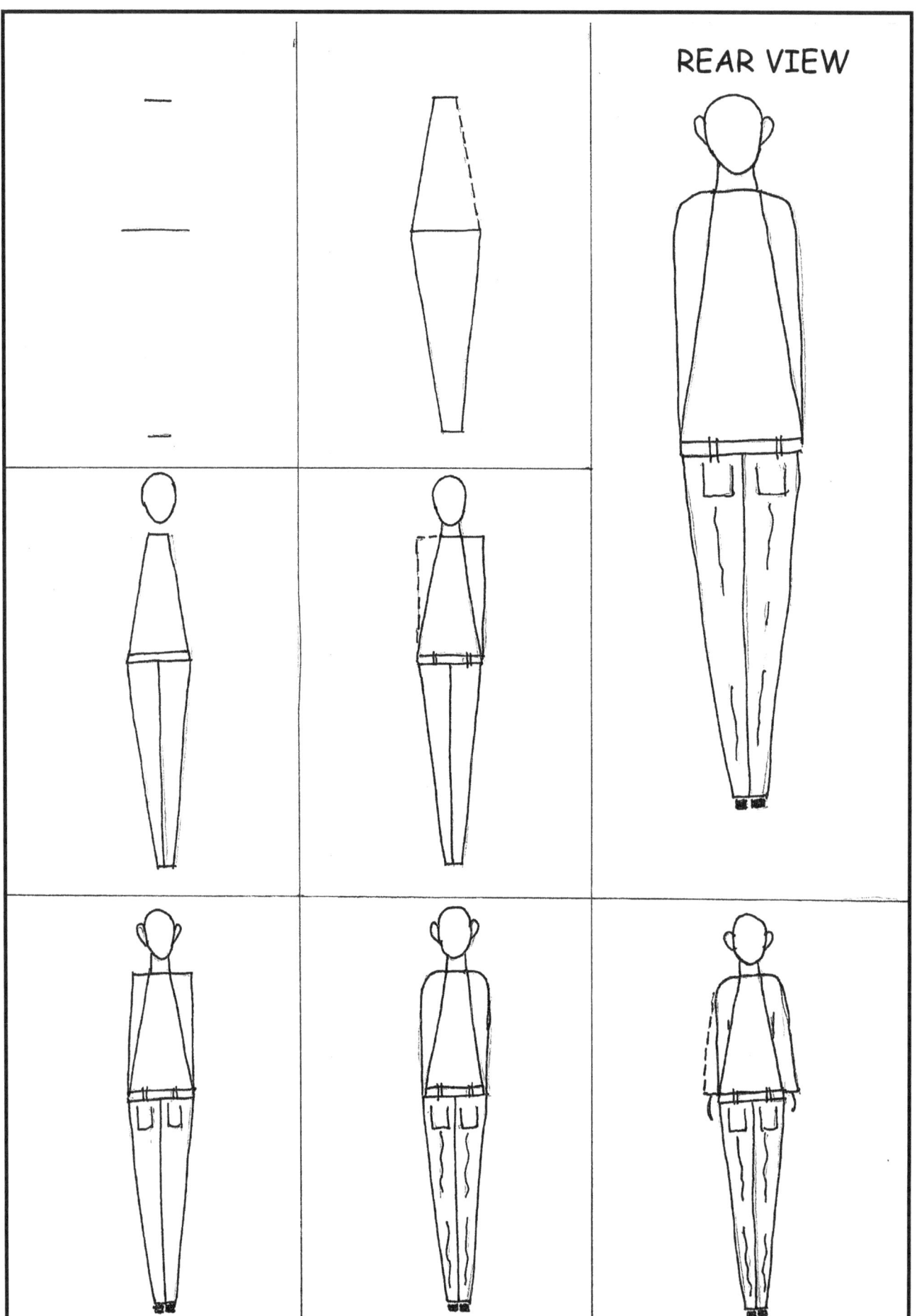

REAR VIEW

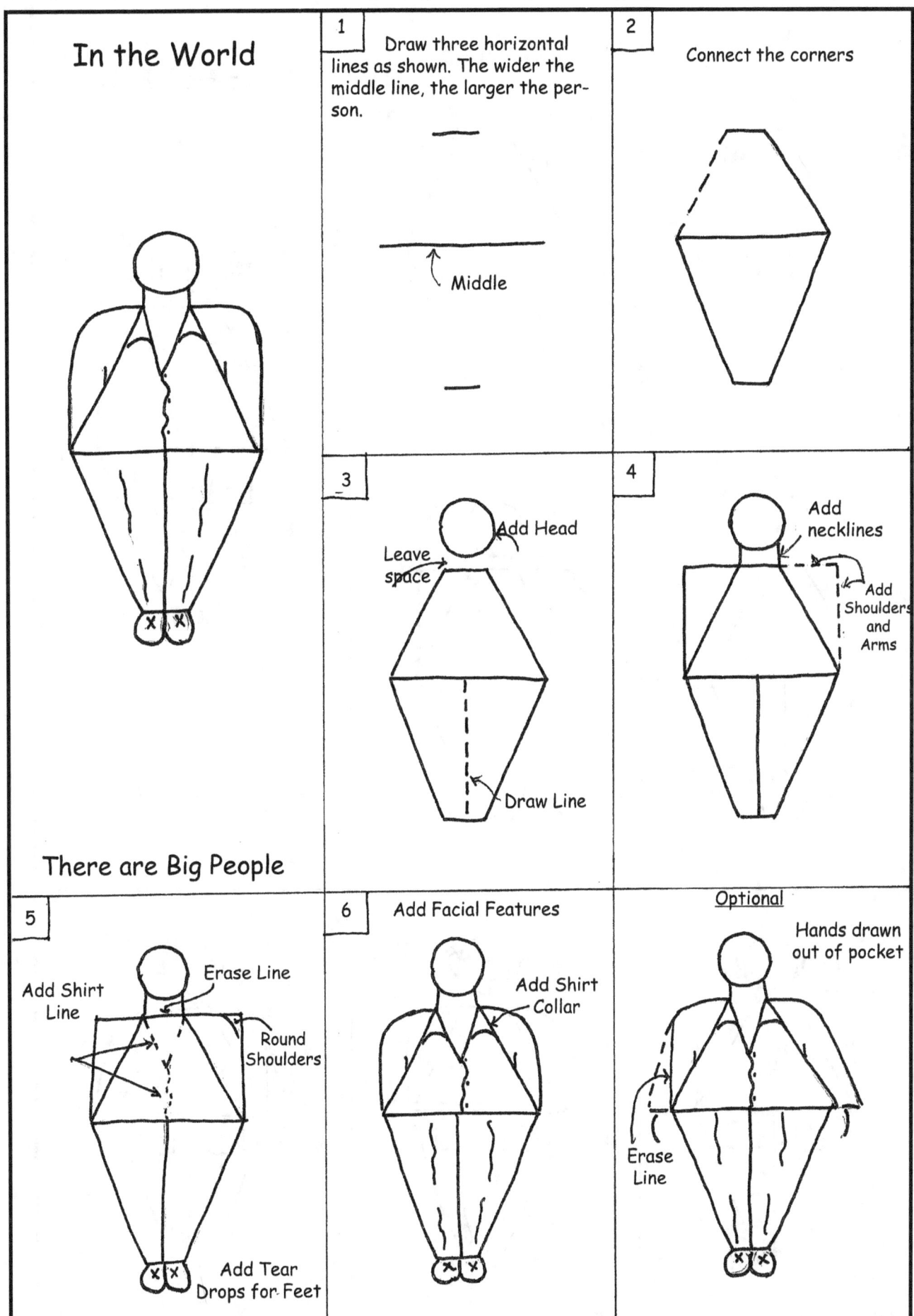

In the World

There are Big People

↖ Middle

2 Connect the corners

3

Leave space →

Add Head ←

Draw Line ←

4

Add necklines

Add Shoulders and Arms

5

Add Shirt Line

Erase Line

Round Shoulders

Add Tear Drops for Feet

6 Add Facial Features

Add Shirt Collar

Optional

Hands drawn out of pocket

Erase Line

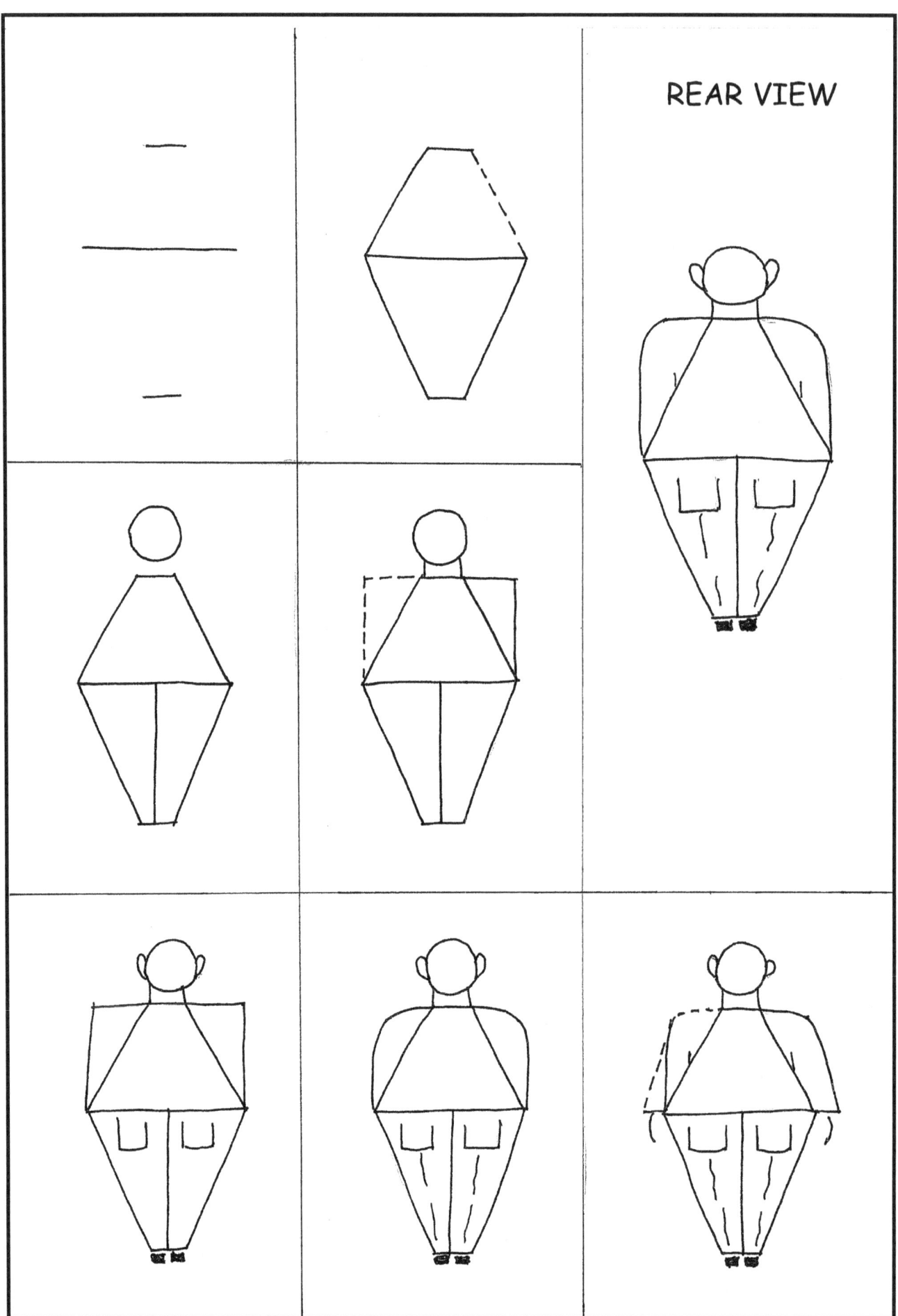

28

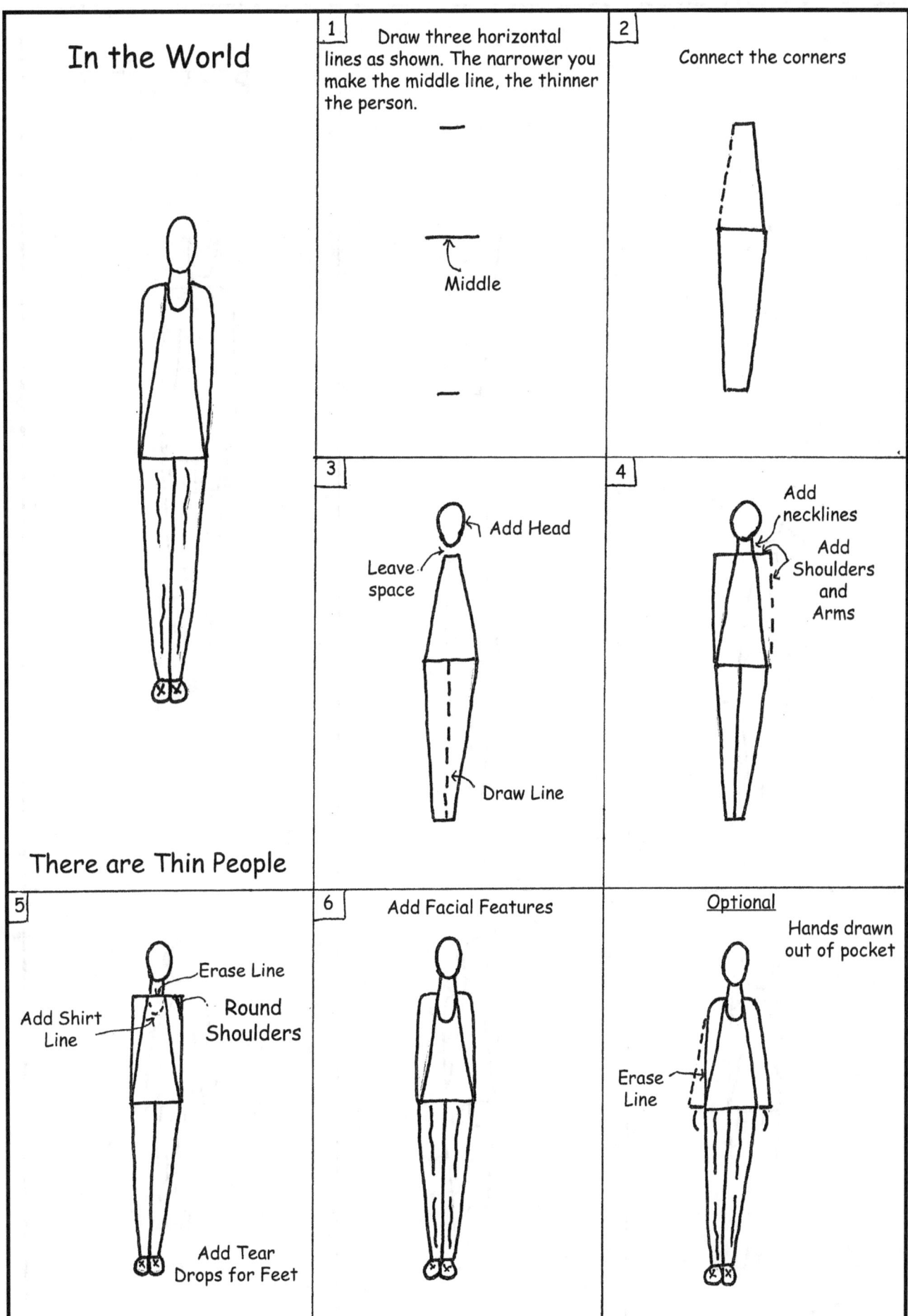

In the World

There are Thin People

1 Draw three horizontal lines as shown. The narrower you make the middle line, the thinner the person.

↑ Middle

2 Connect the corners

3 Add Head

Leave space

Draw Line

4 Add necklines

Add Shoulders and Arms

5 Erase Line

Round Shoulders

Add Shirt Line

Add Tear Drops for Feet

6 Add Facial Features

Optional

Hands drawn out of pocket

Erase Line

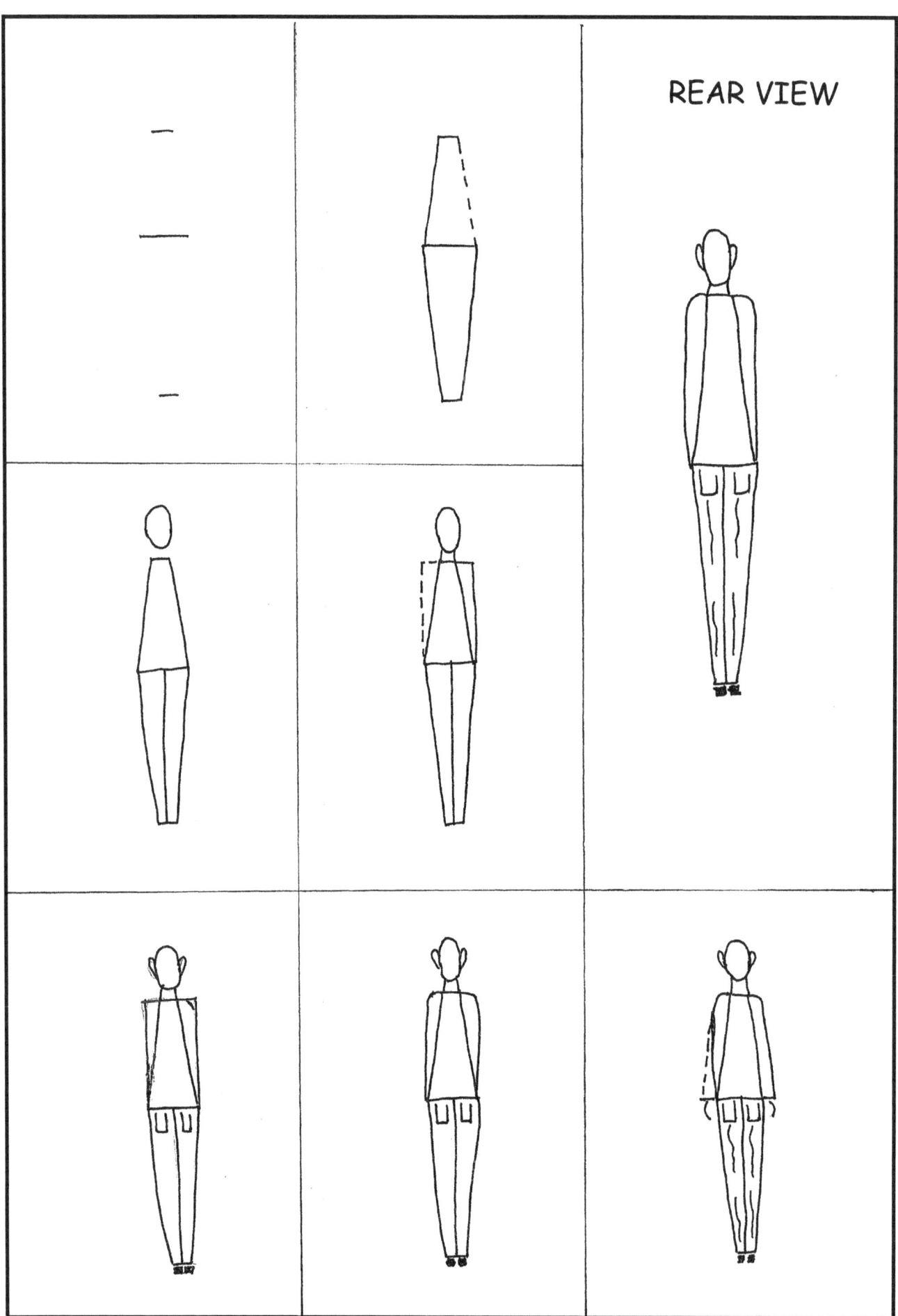

REAR VIEW

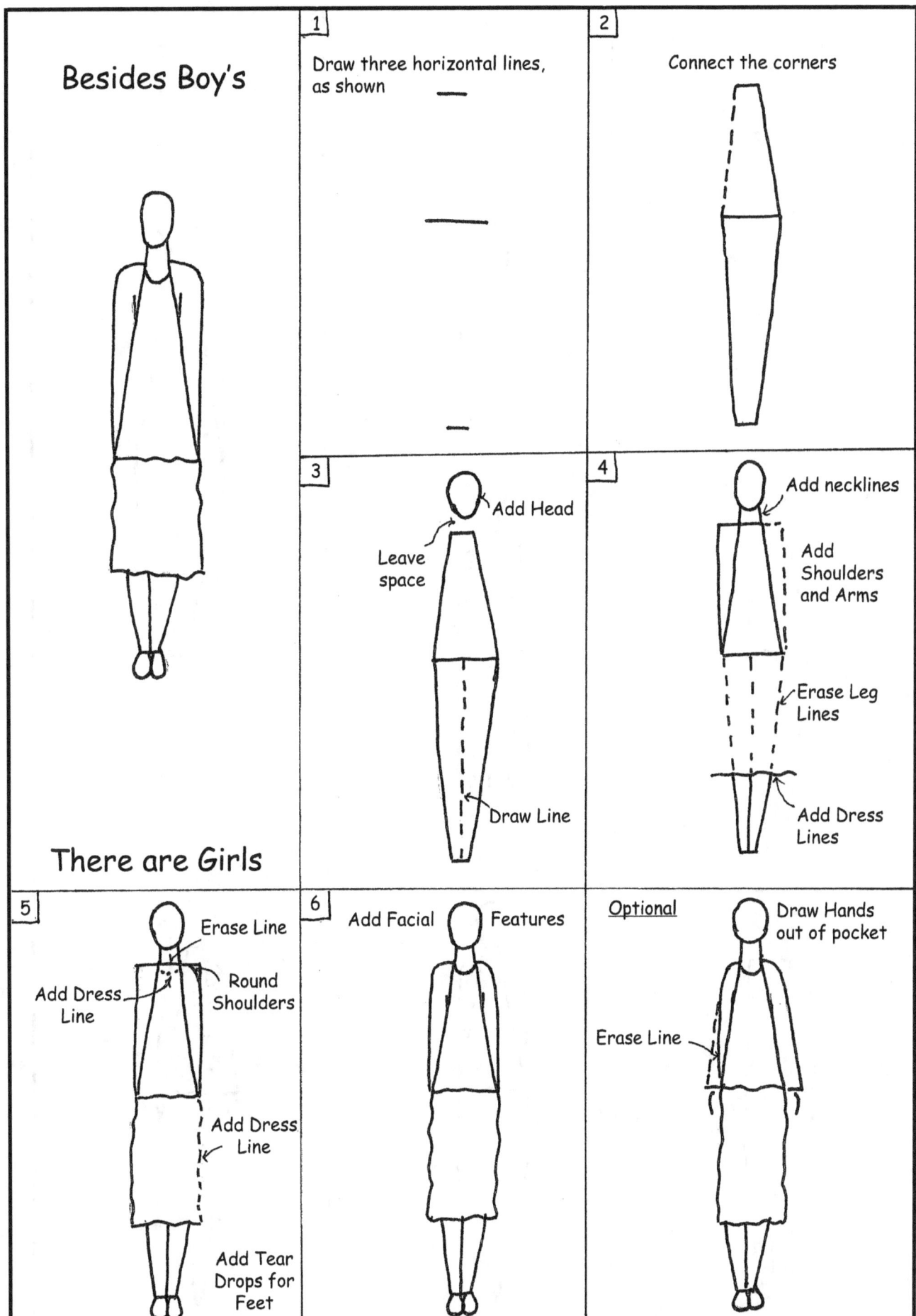

Besides Boy's

There are Girls

1 Draw three horizontal lines, as shown

2 Connect the corners

3 Add Head

Leave space

Draw Line

4 Add necklines

Add Shoulders and Arms

Erase Leg Lines

Add Dress Lines

5 Erase Line

Add Dress Line

Round Shoulders

Add Dress Line

Add Tear Drops for Feet

6 Add Facial Features

Optional Draw Hands out of pocket

Erase Line

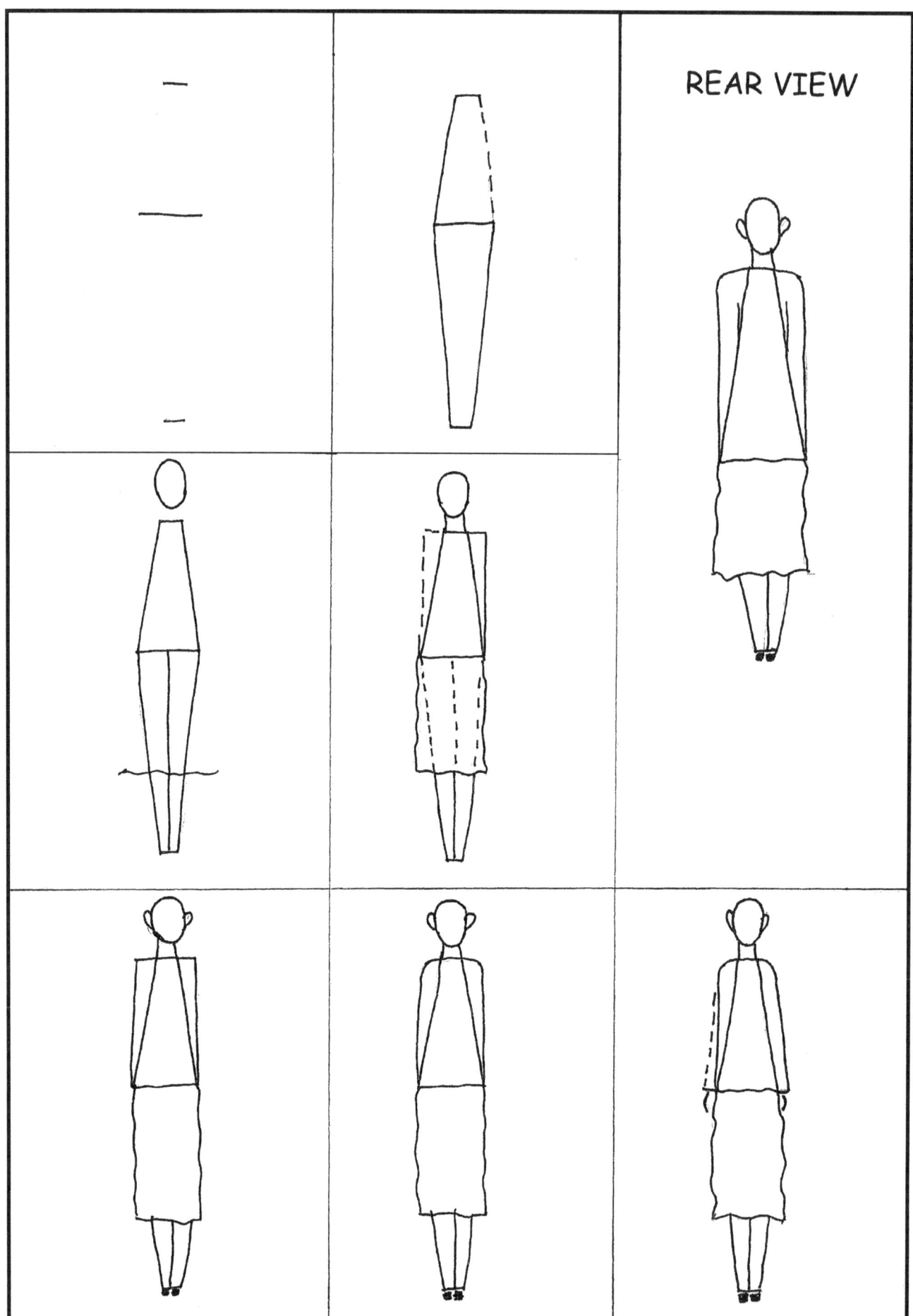

REAR VIEW

Drawing Side Views

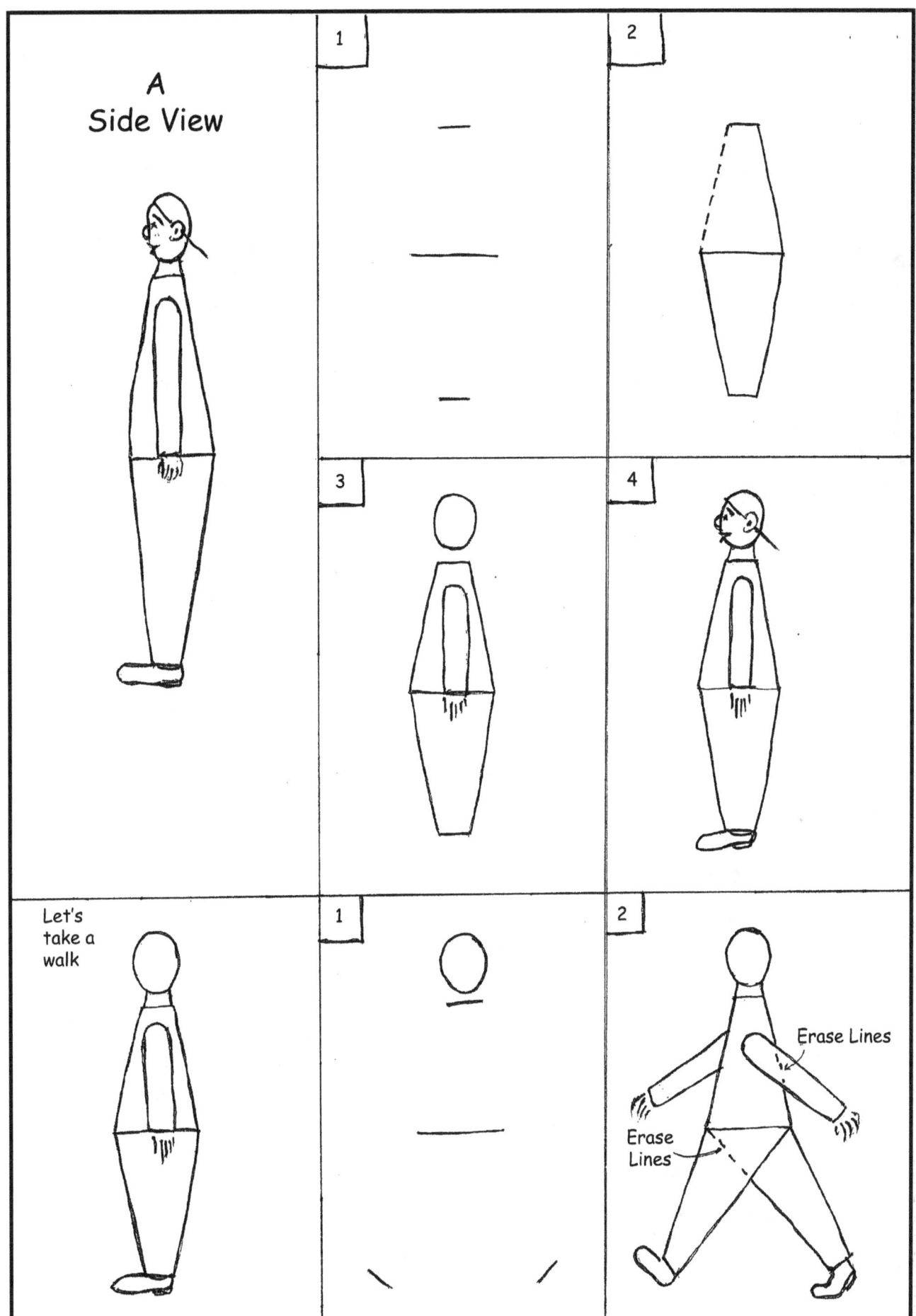

A
Side View

1

2

3

4

Let's
take a
walk

1

2

Erase Lines

Erase
Lines

35

Drawings That Show Motion

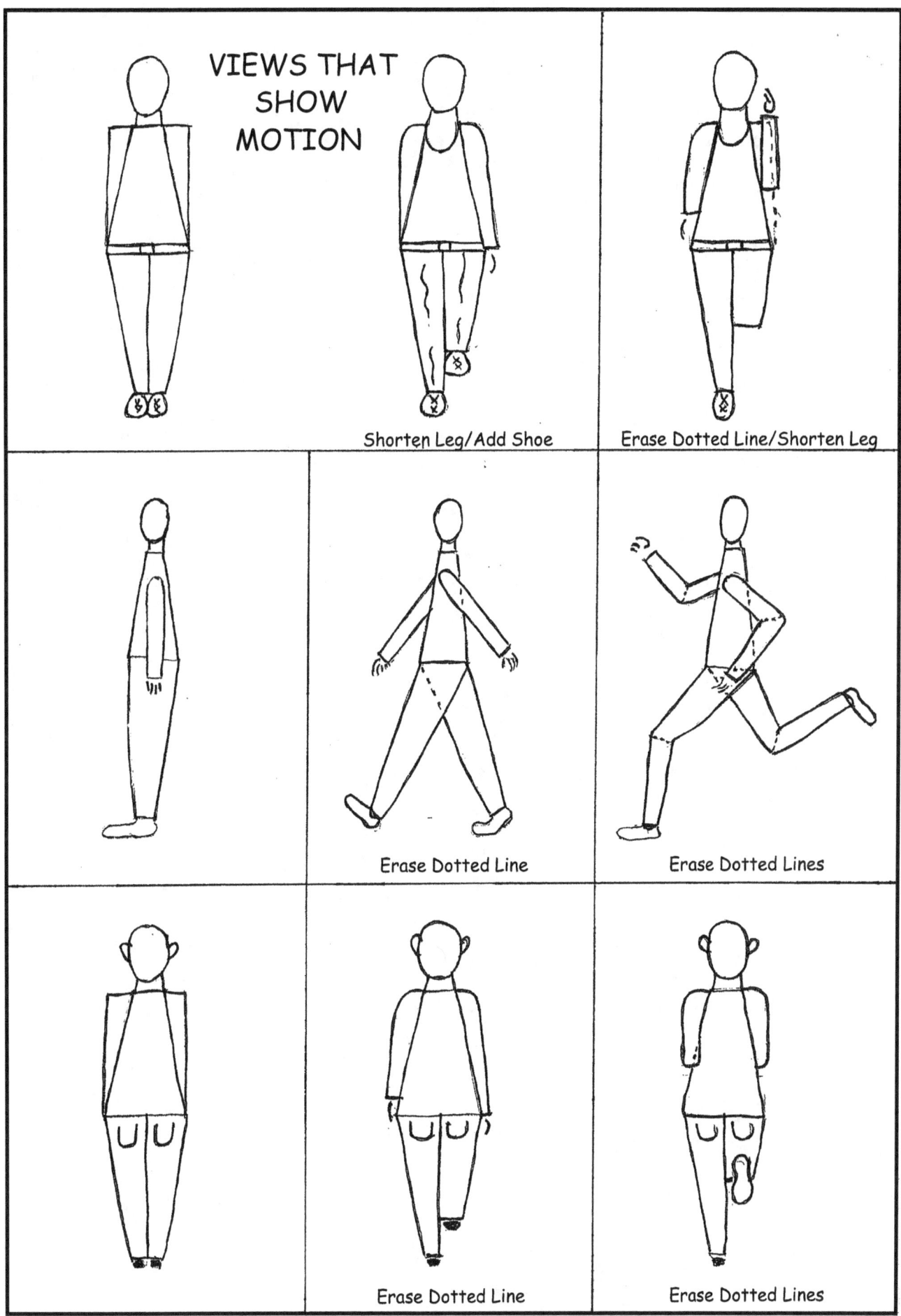

VIEWS THAT SHOW MOTION

Shorten Leg/Add Shoe

Erase Dotted Line/Shorten Leg

Erase Dotted Line

Erase Dotted Lines

Erase Dotted Line

Erase Dotted Lines

Drawing Exercises

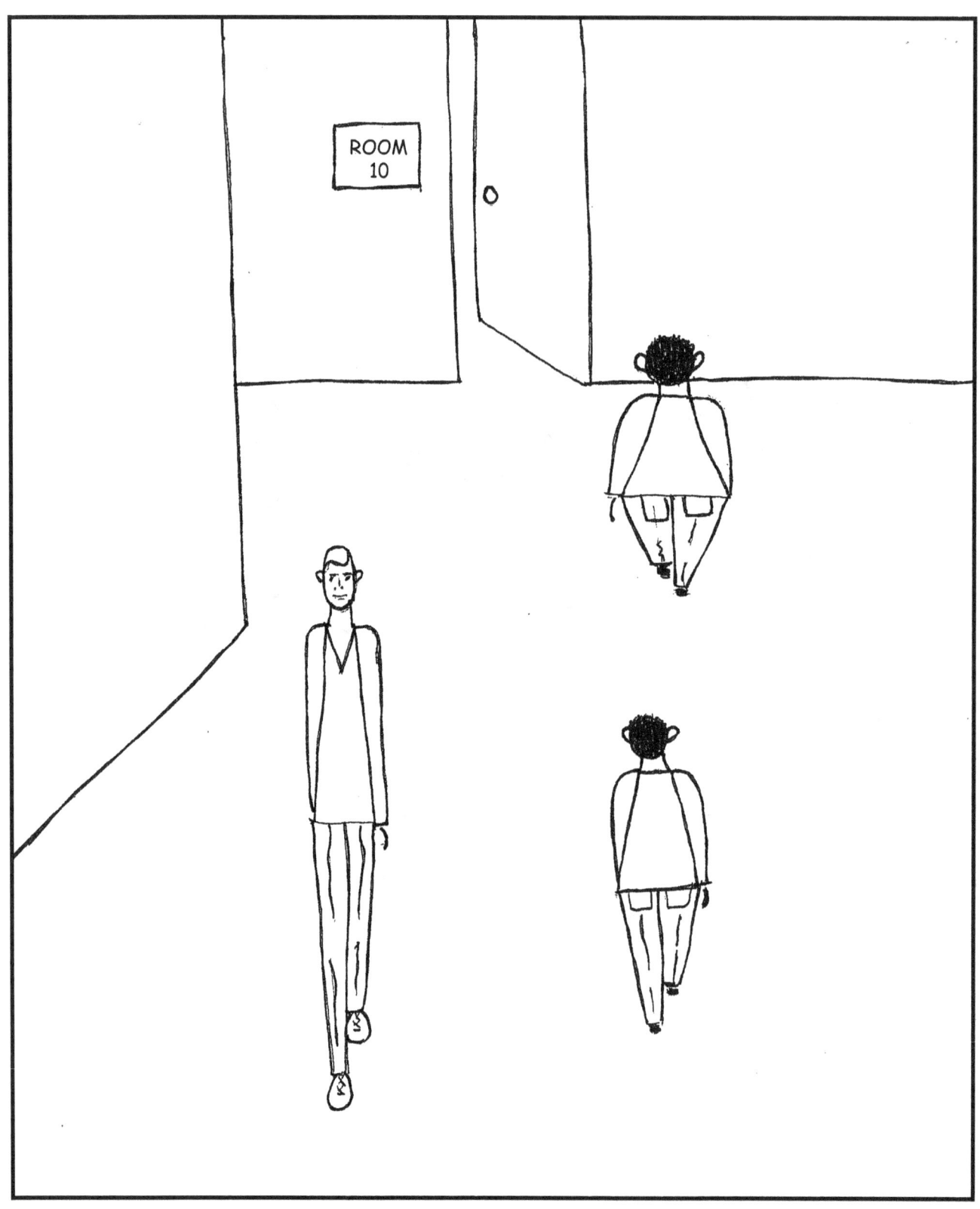

The following are drawing exercises for you. Always draw the
people first. Then the remainder of the drawing.

Practice Space

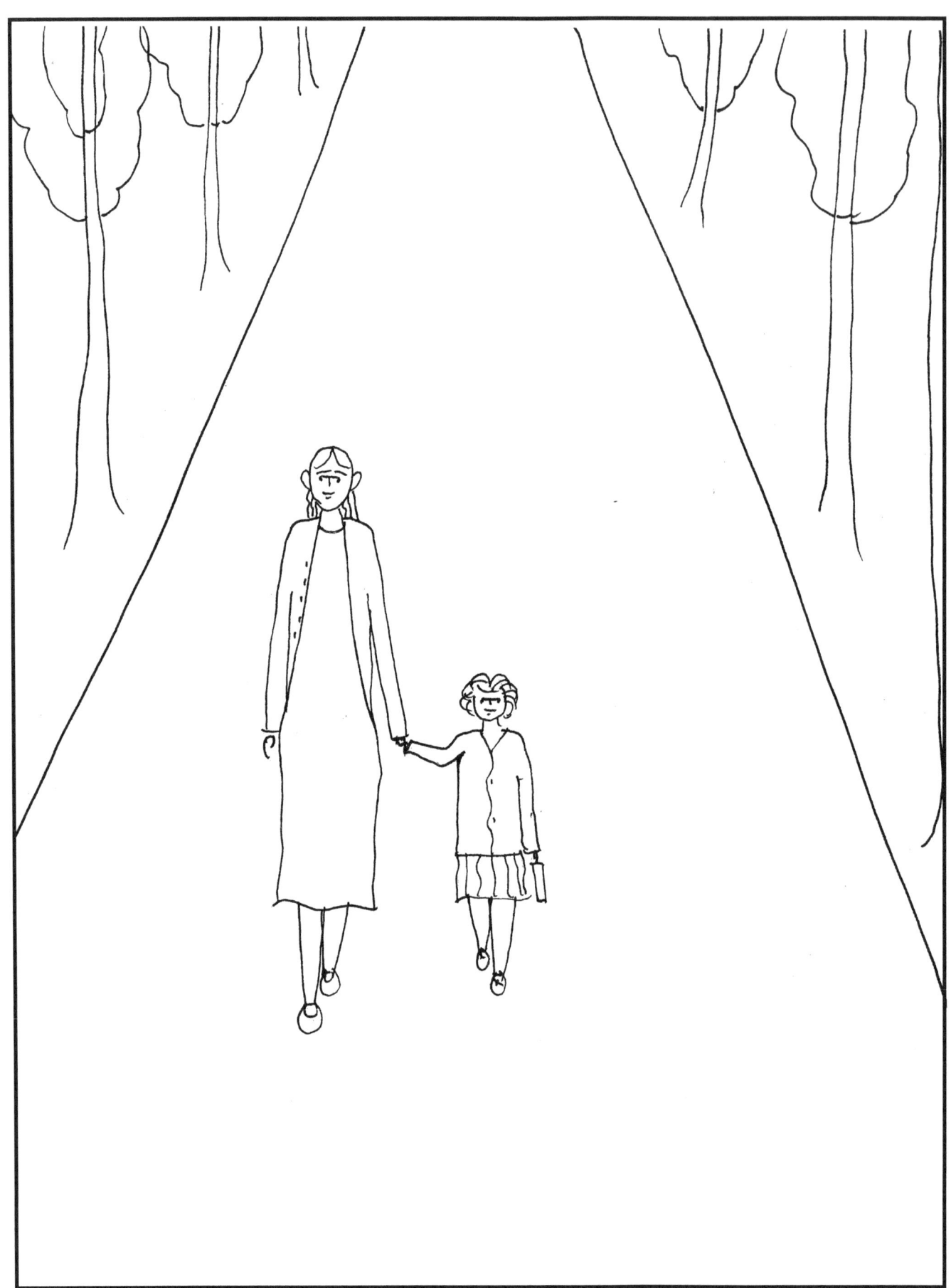

Practice Space

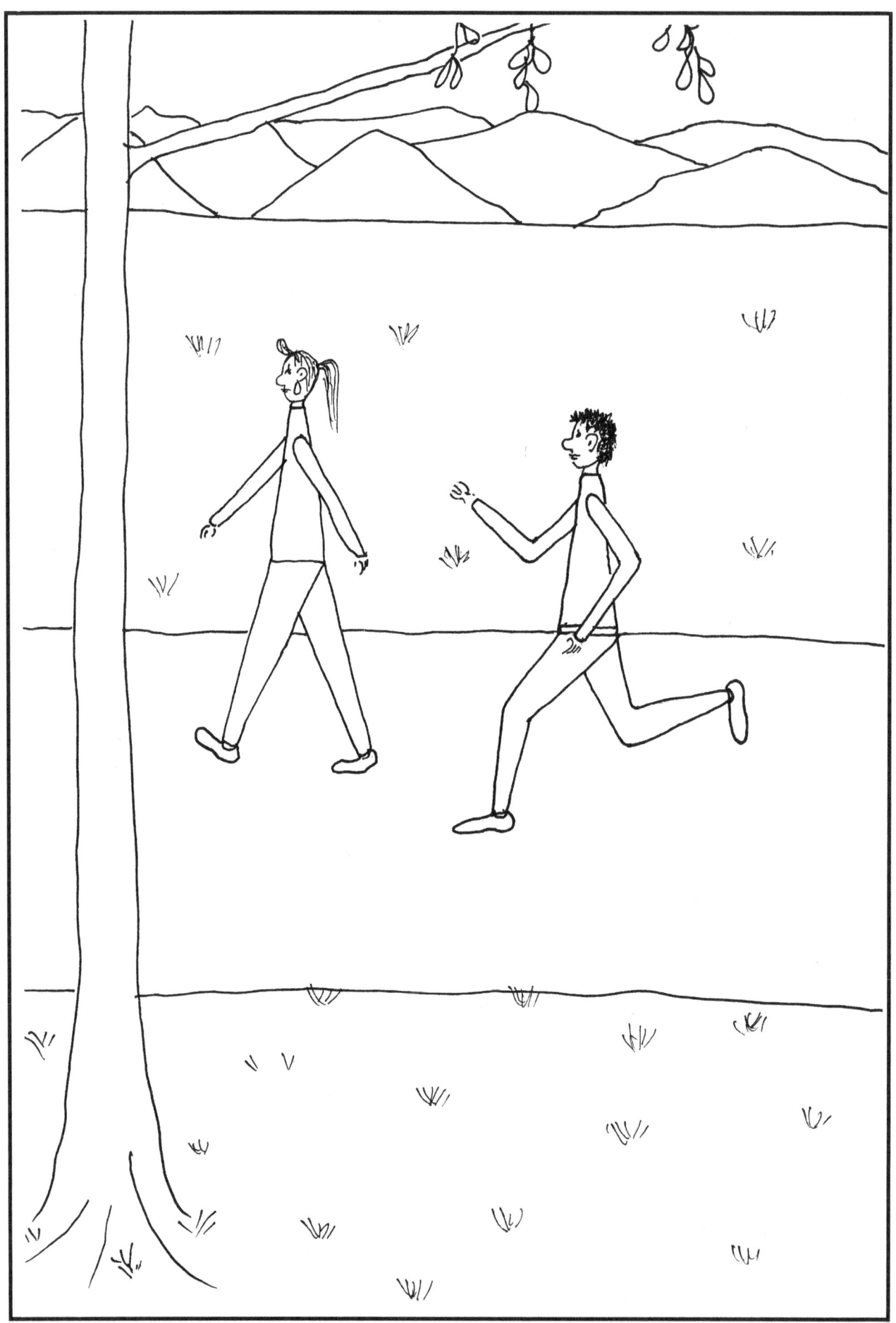

Practice Space

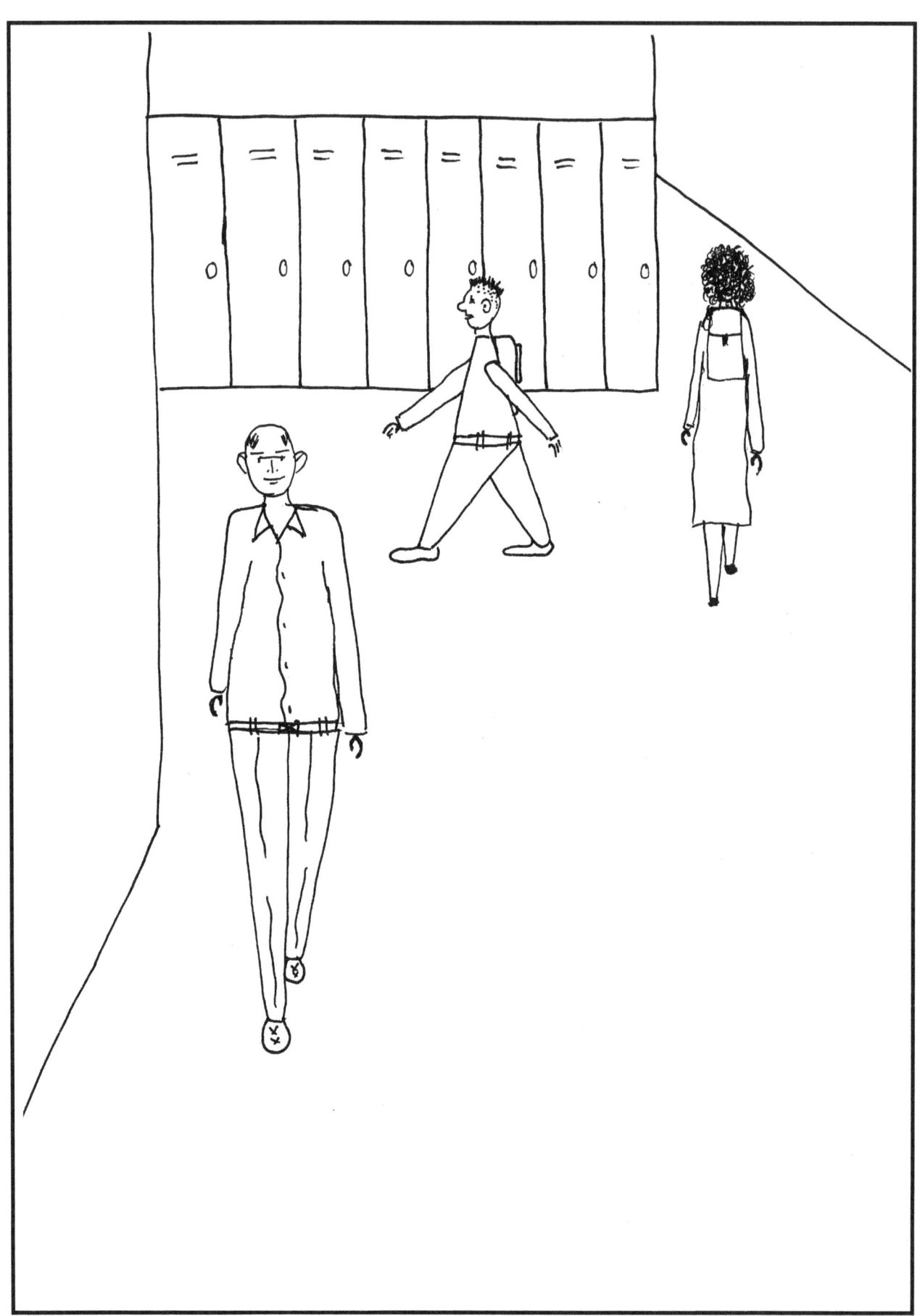

Practice Space

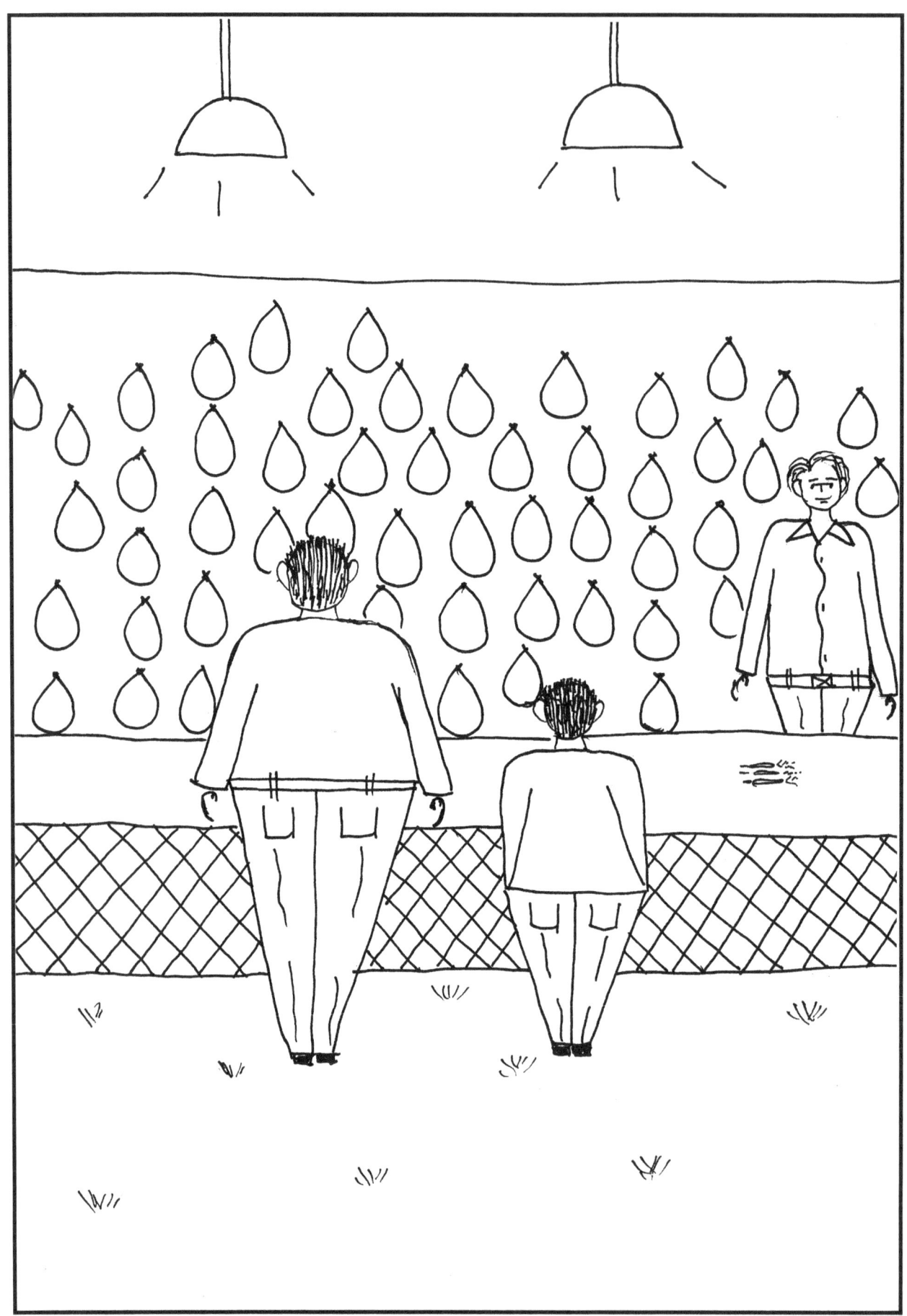

Practice Space

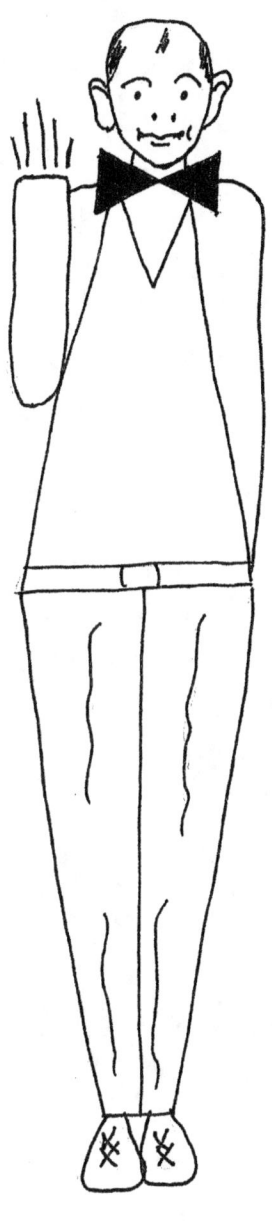

Well,
wasn't that fun!!

I'll be looking
forward to
seeing you again

Good Bye

www.ingramcontent.com/pod-product-compliance
Lightning Source LLC
Chambersburg PA
CBHW081227170526

45165CB00009B/2989